NELLO DAVEY

WORK FROM HOME OPPORTUNITIES

The Ultimate Guide To Work-At-Home Success, Discover Different Job and Work Opportunities That Can Let You Earn Money From Home

Descrierea CIP a Bibliotecii Naţionale a României
NELLO DAVEY
   WORK FROM HOME OPPORTUNITIES. The Ultimate Guide To Work-At-Home Success, Discover Different Job and Work Opportunities That Can Let You Earn Money From Home / Nello Davey – Bucharest: Editura My Ebook, 2021
   ISBN

NELLO DAVEY

WORK FROM HOME OPPORTUNITIES

**The Ultimate Guide To Work-At-Home Success,
Discover Different Job and Work Opportunities That
Can Let You Earn Money From Home**

My Ebook Publishing House
Bucharest, 2021

TABLE OF CONTENTS

WORKING FROM HOME

Working from home is a dream come true for some whose desire is to enjoy the convenience and flexibility that the lifestyle has to offer. The very idea of working from home conjures up ideas of easy living, mid- afternoon naps, and lunch with friends and frequent coffee breaks from their very own coffee makers!

But, although the idea is romantic, the true life of the work at home entrepreneur is anything but romantic. Yes there are the flexible, lazy days, but there is also the realism that no work = no pay.

Working from home is fun and exciting, but only if you are willing to work hard, do your research, market your skills and abilities and put in the necessary time to establish yourself as an expert in your field.

In return for this dedication and hard work, you get to decide your own income level, giving yourself raises as is needed and necessary and yes, you get to take off work when YOU want to.

Most definitely, the ability to create an income from the comforts of home is a very exciting one!

But what is the main reason(s) that so many people are attracted to the very idea of working from home? And why is it that moms and dads are turning in their resignation notices at their stable corporate jobs to pursue those proverbial "pipe dreams" that everyone says they're chasing?

The work at home lifestyle is an attractive one for a number of reasons.

✓ A work at home job offers flexibility

✓ You enjoy a certain level of freedom working from home

✓ There is a convenience working from home and setting your own schedule

✓ You can reduce and eliminate a lot of overhead expenses

Many people are seeking ideas and turning to the draw of the work at home lifestyle as a means of reducing stress (daily commutes, monthly deadlines), reducing their living expenses (taxes, gas, childcare) and finding optional means of creating an income in lieu of the traditional 9-5 fixed corporate work schedules.

Some of these reasons are enough to convince some to even look into it!

And, in addition to the flexibility that the lifestyle creates, the income that can be created is also a draw as well.

The skills and abilities that the work at home entrepreneur possesses give them the opportunity to create a highly competitive income. Their newfound income can rival any corporate salary that they may have once perhaps enjoyed.

In many cases, the only way to experience a spike in your income IS to start your own business, or, greatly reduce expenses and experience an overage in what you payout each month.

Work at home entrepreneurs are often frugal by nature, therefore any momentum that they can build up to help them save money is another draw in itself.

The attraction of a work at home business is so strong, that there is a great pursuit of dreams, hopes and goals that will allow the right kind of person and personality to stay at home, pursuing an income.

If they choose and market the right kind of business for their work at home endeavors, they have the probability to enjoy a strong and residual income for years and years to come.

WHY WORK AT HOME?

Although for some, the answer to that question is pretty obvious, but to others, it may take a little more convincing and persuading to show them the many benefits that they would and can enjoy by being a work at home entrepreneur.

Being and working in a traditional setting like a corporate or manufacturing environment is enough to make a person seriously considering their options and starting their own businesses to think long and hard.

These settings are not necessarily "bad" but are limiting and inflexible to offer the work from home individual what they are seeking and long for - - which is flexibility and convenience.

Gas Savings

One significantly large factor in the work at home issue is the huge savings that you can enjoy on your gas expenses and commute time for work each day.

This expense can significantly increase depending on the distance to and from work on a daily basis and what kind of vehicle is used in the commute.

It is estimated that your average corporate employee spends anywhere from 1-3 hours each day, traveling back and forth to their places of employment. That roughly translates into almost 15 hours per week just in travel time alone!

Coupled with the average 40 hour work week, and that employee is looking at over 50 hours away from home and possibly hundreds of dollars in gasoline and vehicle expense.

Again, those numbers alone is enough to make someone consider the aspects of working from home as a serious consideration!

With working from home, the daily commute can be reduced to as little as 5 minutes to your home office each day. That can significantly reduce the stress associated with daily commutes and traffic stress in traveling on the road.

This one factor alone can also help a stay-at-home parent decide whether or not to brave the corporate world or bounce their little on their knee as they type up their proposals and pitches…from their home office computer.

In addition to the reduction in travel time, you also save on gas expenses as there is no need to use as much, if any, for the five minute commute to your office. Avoiding wear and tear on your vehicle, frequent maintenance and environmental fumes again is a big positive in favor of working from home.

With the fluctuation of gasoline prices and expenses, saving the average family hundreds of dollars a month in gas prices adds to the family budget in a positive way. Instead of worrying about gas for getting back and forth to work, those funds and worries can be placed somewhere else on your agenda.

Availability

As a work at home employee, or more specifically as a work at home parent, you also have the flexibility and the enjoyment of being available to your children as needed. While working from home, you have the option of reducing childcare expenses and carpool expenses for the care of your kids.

If you have the type of business that doesn't interfere with children being around (telephone work, detailed work requiring concentration) than having your children at home with your while you work is ideal.

You get to spend more time with them, experience a lot of "firsts", attend parent-teacher meetings and even help them with their homework after school.

The flexibility that is afforded to you as a work at home parent is a definite plus for a lot of work at home entrepreneurs who deem this as high priority.

However, parents aren't the only people who get to experience perks when they are working from home. There are entrepreneurial-minded people who want their own business, want flexibility and convenience as well, but don't want to have to experience the traditional work environment to be able to enjoy it.

They may be in search of a home business or a work at home job that will give them the best of all worlds and allow them the freedom that the lifestyle affords.

The flexibility to work when you want (in the middle of the night), where you want (on your back deck), and in what you want (pajamas!) is also a draw for those contemplating this flexible lifestyle.

Flexibility

Being in control of your time and being able to do what you want and when you want to is something that many can only dream of. With the right positioning and ideas, you can not only dream but have it as well.

Is flexibility important to you? And convenience as well? With working from home and/or operating a home business, you have the flexibility to work around your family's schedule and other responsibilities as well. What's important to you as a work at home parent?

- ✓ A sick child? You can pick them up from school, bring them home and still continue to work on your proposal.

- ✓ What about vacation time? Schedule it when YOU want to instead of waiting for the office pool to go around, possibly making your request the last one to get approved.

You can take care of errands that can only be handled in the middle of the day and deal with responsibilities that occur within traditional work hours.

Attire/Expenses

What about how you look and what you wear to work everyday? That is a moot issue in the case of the work at home individual. A definite plus for working at home is the reduction in expenses, clothing and accessories that you would incur in a traditional work environment.

There is a very real and often very high expense in maintaining a wardrobe and accessory budget if you have to go out of them home to go to work each day.

The constant need for updating your wardrobe is no longer necessary because you can be as casual as your home business will allow. You can work in your pajamas everyday if you'd like!

Sick Days

Tired of getting sick every time someone at work gets sick? When you work from home, you also reduce your exposure to colds and germs, thereby reducing your chances of missed work days. When you work around other people, there is always the likelihood that you will get sick; that's just the way it is.

Although there is no way that you can completely eliminate germs, especially airborne germs, however working from home allows you to control the exposure that you have to germs and away from those who come to the workplace sick.

Eating Out

Eating out and meals can create a somewhat high expense as well for the traditional worker. Corporate and traditional 8-5 employees eat out almost everyday. Many times, they work near restaurants and eateries that can make it very convenient to go and "grab a bite" while on a quick lunch hour. And with friends, there's an even more enticing reason to spend money eating lunch out. At an average of $5-7 per day for lunch, that can add up to over $1,750 each year spent on eating out!

But, if you working from home, you can save an enormous amount of money on lunches that you eat out. You have quicker access to food that is right at home and you can also make better choices.

It is also more nutritious to eat at home in addition to saving money and curbing costs. You have more control over the types of foods that you eat and also how frequent you eat them.

Exercise

Maintaining an exercise schedule is also a plus for the work at home individual. Want to work out at the gym in the middle of the day? No problem! You can go to your local gym, walk at the park or work out at home on any schedule you'd like since you're able to enjoy flexibility and convenience with your work schedule.

And, since health and exercise is an integral part of a successful work at home plan, you'd be more inclined to do it with flexible opportunities!

With all of the advantages of the work at home lifestyle, there is hard to imagine that there are any disadvantages at all. But, there are. Although the work at home life does offer significant perks and pluses, there are some disadvantages that you may want to consider before you plunge into the lifestyle.

JOIN THE RANKS OF THE ELITE

There are many well-known entrepreneurs who started from their home businesses and became famous with their inventions, ideas and dreams.

Note that although working from home doesn't necessarily dictate success, but one can't help but notice that working from home may perhaps have afforded them a peace of mind that allowed them to comfortably work on their dreams.

Sister Schubert's Rolls

The famous yeast rolls lady who boasts the buttery rolls, blueberry breads and now even cornbread delights started in her own home. Using her kitchen as a test site, Sis. Schubert rolled, baked, tested and delivered yeast rolls right from her kitchen!

She started by operating a home-based catering business called The Sliver Spoon. She used a Parkerhouse rolls style recipe that she got from a family hand-down and the rolls were dubbed "Everlasting Rolls."

Today she has a manufacturing site of course because the business is so huge, but she had the courage and insight to start her empire from her home kitchen and boy are we glad she did!

(more information at http://www.ssrolls.com/home/my-story.dT)

Microsoft Computers

Ever heard of a company called Microsoft or an application called Windows?

What about a man named Bill Gates?

I'm sure you have, but this gentleman, along with a friend started the colossal business known today as Microsoft in their garage! Two little geeky, nerdy guys who were in college deciding to tinker around with some programming, and the rest as they say, is history.

These are just a couple of examples of famous people who have made a living working from their home setting and building businesses that yielded significant attention. With their contributions and their examples, you too have the motivation that it takes to succeed!

Any Disadvantages?

There are, like anything else and anywhere else, disadvantages to to an issue that may seem all-glorious and all wonderful on the surface.

Working at home is not any different, therefore you should really seriously consider the disadvantages that accompany working from home and all that is involved with the lifestyle.

First, consider whether or not you are really ready for the work at home lifestyle that you are considering.

Without all of the romance, the lofty ideas and the pluses that can be misconstrued as generalities, let's look at some very real considerations that you should focus on before you get started in this.

Patience

Do you have the patience and wherewithal that it will take for you to make a go of your business or work at home job until it is self-sustaining?

Do you have the funds and support that you need in order to wait until your income is enough to support you and your family?

Without regards to the perks, consider the time that it will take for you to ramp up your business to create a decent income.

Depending on the type of business that your pursue or the type of company that you go to work for, you may in for a lengthy and/or involved process to get things to where they need to be in order for you to see some progress in that area.

How much of an income do you need to generate in order to live? Sit down and accurately figure out what you need to make on a weekly and/or monthly business before you are ready to embark on a new business idea or venture.

Be realistic in your expectation level and with your expenses. Are you ready to withstand the lean times that will come while you are working towards building that income?

Having a steady income with a traditional job is a definite level of comfort for some individuals. It can be quite unnerving to think that you are responsible for your income, whether you're good at what you do or not. The stability of a guaranteed paycheck from a regular job can quickly become a preference over making the lifestyle of a work at home entrepreneur.

Benefits

Benefits are a very important consideration for the work at home employee. Oftentimes, they have a family to support and need the benefits for them in order to make their lives easier.

You must consider the benefits, or rather the lack of benefits that a work at home individual is without while he or she builds up their income. Benefits can include health and life insurance, dental insurance, paid sick leave and even paid maternity leave.

You should seriously think about NOT having access to these benefits as a contract worker and find out how you can support your family in the absence of them.

Many companies hire freelancers or contractors as a way to avoid paying benefits to their workers. A plus for them, but a minus for you.

Although this is the way *they* save money, you must consider you and your family's health and well being and the security of having medical and dental benefits that they will need while you are pursuing your dream of working for yourself. Can they do without the benefits?

Time

Time is another disadvantage that goes along with the aforementioned schedule and flexibility. One of the drawbacks to consider to having such flexible time, is, having such flexible time.

When you pursue the lifestyle of the work at home person, you also have to consider the amount of time that you will put in and the toll that it takes on the body.

Yes, there is flexibility, but there are also deadlines. And, if there are deadlines to meet with the work at home business, *they must be met*. Whether that is in the middle of the night, with or without a sick child and other responsibilities looming over you to get done, it is up to you to make it all happen.

Time is one of the few commodities that we don't have control over. We all have the same amount of time given to us day in and day out. It's up to us to maximize that time to make everything happen within that time that needs to.

Is the work at home lifestyle for everyone? No, it isn't. But, you should consider the advantages and disadvantage and your own lifestyle before deciding that it is (or is not) something that you would like to pursue.

Of course, it IS a wonderful way to make a living. And, with so many creative, wonderful ways to do it, it's hard not being excited about how everyone can enjoy this lifestyle as well.

Creating Your Success System

As you begin your work from home entrepreneurial journey, you will experience a fair amount of highs and lows as you find out what works for you and what doesn't. The journey towards the lifestyle of working from home is fast, fun, exciting, emotional and often very, very rewarding.

Let's look at some things that you will want to consider and do while you prepare for a lifestyle that will bring you such opportunities and affordability's.

Polish Your Resume

No matter what type of work at home job or business that you plan to pursue, it is advisable to have a current resume ready in case the request ever arises. A well-written resume almost ensures that you get the attention of the right people for the opportunity that you are pursuing.

Keep your resume updated and current. Update your references and skills set as often as needed as well.

As you acquire a new skill or enhance an old one, put it on your resume!

Your current and skills-in-process contribute greatly to any consideration that you would get as a home-based worker or contractor. Working from home is no reason to not be as polished or professional as you would be in a corporate setting.

When you are assembling your resume, list all of your applicable skills and experience that are pertinent to the type of business that you are pursuing.

➤ Are you efficient in data entry work?

➤ Do you have a very pleasant and inviting telephone or marketing persona?

➤ Are you multi-degreed, have a skill or technical knowledge that is hard-pressed to find?

Every type of business experience and exposure helps to present you as the polished professional that you'd like to be considered as having.

Since attracting clients and potential employers is a key aspect for your business, you want to present yourself in a positive, professional manner.

Also, verify and confirm the references that you have listed on your resume. There is a possibility that your potential employers and clients may contact them for a personal reference or a character reference.

Make sure their contact information is correct and current and also that you still have their permission to use them as a reference.

Preparing your resume can be as easy as typing up a Word processing document. Although resumes today are communicated via the Internet through email communications and within online portals, they still need to be as polished as can be.

Perform spell checks and grammar checks to ensure that they flow correctly. Have a professional peer scan your resume for consistencies and to make sure dates and descriptions are correct as well.

There are many resume templates available within several word processing documents that will help you in outlining how the resume will look, how it will flow, and how detailed or thorough it needs to be.

There are also resume help services that will help you to develop your resume and polish it professionally enough to gain a lot of attention.

These services can range widely in prices, but the price can be offset by the results that you get from having such a professionally-presented resume.

Just determine beforehand how you want your resume to look and sound since it's unlikely that you will be changing it on a frequent basis.

Carve out your work space

Working from home will be the perhaps the best decision that you've ever made. However, *where* you work when you are working from home will be the second most important decision that you're going to make.

Depending upon the nature of your work and how frequently you need access to your computer, you will be spending a lot of time in front of your computer system all day and will need to establish a quiet, comfortable area to get everything done that you need to get done.

Your workspace should be sufficient enough to provide you with the comfort and capabilities that accompany long, hard-working days.

Email communications

Have a dedicated email address that is separate and distinctly set up for outside communications with potential clients and questions to/from customers.

This will help you keep the professional touch that you need and enable you to also keep all of your pertinent business information in one spot for easier access.

Work Schedule

Determine the hours that you are able to devote to your home business. Setting the hours well in advance will help you work smart and eliminate any time wasters (social networking, phone calls, etc.) and focus intently on your daily responsibilities.

Since working from home is such a wonderfully flexible lifestyle, it is far too easy to get caught up in putting off responsibilities until later or not doing them at all. This can eventually become harmful and damaging to your attempt to meet deadlines and continue on a productive work schedule.

Update your computer software

Updating your computer software regularly helps your computer run more efficiently and more effectively. Your software can detect computer viruses and any technical problems that can be a threat to your system.

When you are working from home, it is important that you have the most currently available software for your system to ensure that you have optimal productivity.

Run regular and systematic computer scans and turn your computer off at night if possible.

Back up your files at least once a week (or more if you have a super-busy business) to ensure file retrieval if there is ever a problem.

Also, since computer viruses are very common and rampant, ensure that you have the latest and the most efficient software to guard against a virus infiltrating your system.

WORK AT HOME SCAMS: DUE DILIGENCE

Work at home scams are very prevalent in the work at home community and run rampant on sites that make wide, bogus promises. As a work at home pursuer, you are going to be targeted from the likes of these bunches and become inundated requests and appeals that often look and sound fake from the beginning!

When you decide that you want to work from home, you may want to begin an extensive online research campaign to find out which business will work best for you.

Since they are so elusive yet prevailing, you really need to have a sharp eye to be able to detect what is a scam, what is real and what is blatantly illegal and needs to be avoided at all costs.

You may visit several online websites and forums that promise "easy money" or that will make you a "millionaire in 90 days." Of course, these claims are preposterous, but there are companies who do make these claims.

Work at home businesses cloaked as scams are tricky and often hard to detect. They may look and sound legitimate yet have all of the elements of a bad business transaction and promises on impending wealth that just aren't ever going to manifest.

What are some of the characteristics of a scam that you should watch for?

✓ Promises to get rich in a short amount of time. Usually 30 days or less is what these places will promise that you can gain thousands if not millions of dollars.

✓ No work required. Really? There is nothing legal where you can make money and not put forth any effort. Exaggerated claims are the hallmark of most every type of scam.

✓ No real business address. Often these addresses have P.O. Boxes or addresses that cannot even be Googled.

✓ No contact information. Who is the person or persons that you need to contact for more information? If you can't find them on the website, chances are that they don't exist.

When you begin seeking out potential job offers or opportunities, there are companies who are targeting those who are just like you; eager, inquisitive and maybe even desperate to find work that will let them enjoy the work at home lifestyle.

They target those with these emotions because they know that they are likely to want more information and are likely to buy what they're selling.

If you know what to look for on a site and know what questions to ask, you can avoid having problems and disasters that can set you back from pursuing your quest to become a home business owner.

So how can you spot a work at home scam and bypass them to get to the legitimate information?

Stay clear of websites or job posting opportunities that require a registration or a membership fee to receive their job posting information.

Much of the information that they have posted on their website is readily available for free over the Internet. They may be charging you a fee for nothing.

These sites are systematically preying upon those who have a desire to work from home but may perhaps lack leads and/or more information on how they can get started. They even seem to be able to directly target how you're feeling, what you're thinking and may even propose to know what type of financial condition you're in.

Oftentimes, the scammer will give information and "testimonials" on other successful work at home opportunists in an effort to secure your trust and get you to ask for more information about their program.

These testimonials are often paid and/or scripted just in order to get you to believe the story that's behind them. They are not true.

They target college students, work at home moms, the retired or unemployed, giving them real life scenarios and preying on their emotions of wanting more income and becoming debt free.

They will share how these everyday people can go from making little to no money can become millionaire in no time at all.

There are pictures of the grandest wealth; beautiful cars, homes, Olympic-sized swimming pools, rolling estates, the finest foods and clothes. The scam sites know that this is appealing to many who want to work at home and will use this to their ultimate advantage.

When the only thing that the average aspiring home worker wants is to have a few things that will make their lives easier, they look at those pictures and may start to believe they can have it. The promises and the ability to gain this massive wealth is what the deft scammers promise them. They're very clever in their presentations and promise so much more if you respond and/or take action now. In exchange for one thing…

Your credit card number!

These outrageous claims of financial success make the recipient believe that they can enjoy all of the perks and things that come with the opportunity if they simply act immediately on the offer.

They make the offer so irresistible that it would be hard to pass it up, right?

But, what's the *real* truth?

Those wildly outrageous claims of instant wealth with little work and little investment are all completely false. There is absolutely no way that an individual can ever make the insane amount of money that the commercial is advertising!

One clue is the fine print that should be posted (albeit elusively) at the bottom of the website's page. There is fine print there for a reason: they don't want you to read it therefore they make it extremely difficult to do so.

Read the disclaimer that is posted and you will see that not only are "results not typical" but they are also "not a guarantee" of what you would and could make in the program. This is your guarantee that not only will you NOT make this kind of money, but that it's likely that you also won't make very near it either.

Another clue of the well-crafted scam is a timed clock that may be on the site. There may be a rush for you to make a decision before 'time runs out'.

This is a sales pressure tactic that is designed to get you to make a quick, emotional, on the spot decision without considering the consequences. In other words, they are trying to get you to buy before you realize what you've done or what you've bought.

They're using emotional tactics and pressure points to get you to do this.

Since making a split second decision works to their benefit, they are not in the least concerned about what harm, financial or otherwise, will do to you. If you do let this pressure work on you, you will sorely regret it later AND have financial penalties to show for it.

In reality, the deal that has such a time-sensitive deadline attached to it will still be available even when you come back to it later. If you don't believe that, leave the site and come back within 24 or 48 hours and you will see that the appeal is still there!

Therefore, it is highly advise that you take the necessary time to thoroughly and effectively check out the deal and the claims that the site is proposing if you only "act now."

Additionally, you can guard against the scam that the site is forging by simply doing your homework. Just take them time to evaluate what the business is and what is really being offered.

❖ Is the business idea a novel one?

❖ Is the sale price of the offer a reasonable price?

❖ Does the business require a down line or for more people to join?

Often, the business idea doesn't have anything that is significantly different or special that would require your immediate action or that you pay enormous amounts of money that can't wait until you can comfortably check them out.

To find out more information about the company, you can also type their name into the Google search engine and see what information you can derive.

The search engine will usually return several instances of where the company's name appears and in what context they are discussed.

Check online forums and chat rooms to see what others are saying about the company and to also see if there are any complaints about the way they do business.

- ✓ Have there been any recent complaints about their services?

- ✓ Are they registered with the Better Business Bureau, online or offline?

- ✓ Are there any genuinely satisfied customers? What are they saying?

So, when you sign up for those work at home business opportunities, what do you typically get that will change your life and make you rich overnight?

Sometimes, all you may receive is an ebook that contains general information that really is of no value to you. Again, it may be information that is readily found on the Internet or maybe information that is not too particularly enlightening in any fashion.

And, it may be teaser information that is just to get you to sign up other opportunity seekers just like yourself, thereby gaining your newfound wealth from their inquisitiveness and response to your business pitch.

There really isn't anything new that you can expect, except the same tricks reprocessed and repackaged to get you to believe that there is something different. Scammers are clever and have taken the time they need to perfect their craft.

The only real thing that you will receive is frustration and anxiety from the likes of these scammy type businesses. These companies will target you to try and get you to buy something or buy into something that is ethically dishonest and will make you pennies, at best.

Although it's questionably dishonest, the only way to make money with the scam is to recruit other opportunity seekers that are just like you. Once you recruit them, you earn a commission for each interested sign up that you get.

Unfortunately, many work at home individuals buy into this thinking ad work hard to convince others that the program can be the answer to their financial troubles. Desperation often ensues.

The opportunity seekers will then tout and herald the program in most any venue where he can. He simply wants to recoup his lost money to try and get back his lost investment.

There are sometimes scolding claims that the recipient did not follow the rigid and obscure guidelines, therefore that is why they did not make the windfall of money that the system promises.

These excuses given by these work at home business opportunities providers are an attempt to deflect responsibility, placing the blame and lack of any money-making abilities on the backs of the opportunity seekers.

The fine print disclaimer essentially dissolves any legal responsibility that the owner may otherwise have, thereby alleviating him of any fiscal responsibility to refund you or even to make good on the program.

This is why it is excruciatingly important to follow good advice, read the fine print, ask tough questions and walk away if the opportunity just doesn't seem quite right. Spending money only to find out that you were fooled and tricked is not only humiliating but financially draining as well.

Watch out for ads that are often disguised in the form of legitimate jobs. These are often used on job search sites to get unsuspecting interested parties to sign up. They will use all sort of tactics and tricks to solicit credit card numbers and financial information.

Don't think that large job search sites are immune either! Read the fine print on the big-promising ads. Many of them will tell you that they do not actually offer jobs but instead access to some database.

Keep detailed records of jobs sites and places where you apply. Don't forget to include the company's name, your contact person's name, the date you applied, the web site, and any important information about the company that you will need to refer back to later.

This little procedure will save you a lot of headache and angst in the long run. You can save a lot of time in searching the web site when it's necessary. It also allows for easier follow-up with the company to find out the status of your application and what other information you need to know. It also helps when remembering what you applied for when you finally receive an answer at a later time.

Keep applying for jobs that allow you to work from home, and apply for things as much as you can and as often as you can. The more your resume is visible and accessible, the higher are your chances of finding a job that suits you and fits your lifestyle.

Very often, these online companies will take months to give you an answer on the status of your resume or application, so don't get discouraged. This is not a sign of your abilities, but is often more internal and indicative of the company.

40

The variety of the type of work at home jobs that are available will be very helpful in narrowing your search for finding a job that is appealing to you.

Always apply for a mixture of various jobs so that you will not be dependent on one company's answer or waiting on one decision.

DISSECTING A WORK AT HOME OFFER

The work at home community is a veritable breeding ground for scams and the likes of them. There are false job offers and claims that claim they will help you build your home business. There are offers of free money and even offers of finding legitimate work at home jobs with little or no money or time investment.

How are these jobs so elusive and plentiful? Most of them are disguised as legitimate job offers or businesses that have a legitimate sounding business model.

Whether they're offering a product or service, they have a way of making it sound very real and very doable for the average, everyday person.

However, there are some businesses and people in business who use legitimate business places as a front for scam operations. But in order to separate the legitimate jobs from the false jobs requires diligence in time and in research.

Take note that whenever you are notified via phone or email that you have received a job or position that you didn't even apply for, it is undoubtedly a scam. Many of these unsolicited offers originate from unknown sources... these offers are never legitimate.

How do they do it?

The scammers peruse job search sites, seeking any pertinent information about you, often posing themselves as a potential employer. They know that this will get your attention.

They do this by browsing the database of the forums job searches looking for people who are looking for jobs.

They know that these people are in need of money, an income, and they pose themselves as being the source with that information.

Once they have your email addresses, they then pitch the fake job offer and just sit back and wait for you to either provide them with your credit card information or provide them with even further personal information so that they can continue to send you more job appeals for work that doesn't exist.

The only thing that you can do to guard against being caught in this type of scam is to immediately delete the job offers as you get them.

You should never respond to them, as this action will simply be notification that your email address is valid.

Therefore, there will continue to be more job offers, more appeals and more annoying emails. Deleting them and NOT responding will often discourage them from sending even more appeals.

Also, these email lists are often sold to other scam operation companies who buy email lists. The cycle begins again with the company who purchases your name and email address.

Another red flag that a scam is a scam is the inflated pay per hour that they post on their site. In common sense thinking, there is no company, online or offline, who will pay a contractor an exorbitant hourly rate to do mundane tasks like answer the telephone or perform Internet searches.

There *will* be gigs that will land you a nice, lucrative income, but those will have a certain level of expectation and require a certain skill level to match.

If you get any offer for jobs that are fake, false or that ask for your personal financial information, you can report these places to the Internet Crime Complaint Center. They state on their website that they are affiliated with Federal Bureau of Investigations (FBI) and National White Collar Crime Center. Reporting this false offers will help reduce the number of scammers who are posting them.

OPPORTUNITIES TO AVOID

There are other online scams that the work at home business person needs to steer clear of and watch out for. Often, these scams portray as harmless, but in reality they are very dangerous and can be damaging to any efforts that you have put towards working from home in a successful capacity.

Lotteries

How many times in one month have you won the lottery? Dozens probably. The lottery, especially the British Lottery, claims that their recipients win in pounds, and in millions of them.

This not only is untrue, but there are emails constantly being sent to unsuspecting online opportunity seekers saying that the recipient has won an exaggerated amount of money.

This can be especially tempting to respond to if as a business opportunity seeker, you are looking for the next big money-making venture that will give you an unlimited income potential.

Rest assured knowing that these particular types of lotteries that arrive in your email in-box announcing instant riches is a scam. They work very swiftly and very adeptly, asking you to pay fees to transfer the money out of the country it is in.

Once you fall for this scam the first time, they continue asking for more and more assistance with transferring the money.

They also continue asking for higher and higher fees transfer amounts, promising you reimbursement and additional money for your time and inconvenience.

Because everything moves so swiftly, you can be swindled out of a lot of money before you realize what is happening.

When all is said and done, it is horrific to realize that not only are you now broke, but you will also never recover the money that you used as fees to transfer money for this overseas company. Why? Because the company was fake…it never existed.

Money Transfers

Another similar type of job offer that is like the lottery is one that is done via email and where you are asked to perform a financial transaction. The scammer will say that they need representatives or financial offers to complete particular transactions in the United States.

They will claim that without your help, this transaction cannot be accomplished. However, the proposed transaction has a lot of nuances to it that suggest illegal activity as well as immoral and illogical behavior.

They will begin by asking you to transfer money from their clients to your bank account with a check, a money order, or through a wire transfer.

They give you complete instructions on how to do this and give you a deadline time as well to ensure that the transaction takes place within their referenced time (possibly a window of time that avoids them getting caught).

If you are in agreement with this and consent to comply with their request, you then move on to the next step and then things begin to get somewhat complicated.

You then transfer the money that they've asked you to hold for them into another bank account. Deducting a generous percentage that you keep for yourself, you then forward the balance of the money on to the recipient immediately.

This whole scenario sounds like it would be and is an incredibly easy way to make fast cash and create a source of income for you. However, the check, the money order and the wire transfer are all fake, but unfortunately you will not find this out until after the transactions are completed.

When the money initially appears in your account, everything looks, sounds and feels legitimate for what you've been asked to do.

You have followed all of the instructions and transferred the money out of your account. But a few days later, you have noticed that the checks that you have deposited now bounce and you are now liable for those amounts.

You are also now liable for any bank fees that incur as a result and you also find out that the bank will become quite aggressive in recovering their fees in recouping their losses. Things have become a nightmare for you.

With banks and lending institutions, all losses are the responsibility of the person's name on the bank account and any other issues that arise out of financial negligence. The bank is only interested in getting their money back.

If the money cannot be recouped and unable to be repaid, there is a chance then that criminal charges can be pressed, and in many cases often is.

Without having realized it, you were a participant in a money-laundering scheme. You were duped out of a significant amount of money and there isn't anything, or very little, that you can do about it.

Multi-level Marketing or MLM

Almost all multilevel marketing businesses are scams and have scam potential. Multilevel marketing, or more widely known as a MLM, is a type of work at home business that is similar to pyramid schemes.

Initially, a person becomes an affiliate of a product or service, sometimes using it themselves in order to make it more credible or more believable. Along with the recommendation to use this product or service, they solicit their friends and family to sign up as affiliates and use them as well.

The person who initiated the affiliated business will make money off the product or service sale and also reap a percentage of the fee that their referred affiliate paid. Sadly, many people do not make money from this venture and only the person at the very top will profit.

Before you consider investing any money into these types of business setups, investigate the originators of the multilevel marketing business. Simply run a search on your favorite search engine and clue in to any information that returns form the site's name.

To limit the search, enter the owner's name and the name of the company along with the word "scam". This may result highly and bring hidden search results to the surface.

There may also be that the company's owner may be involved in more than one business. This is one of the most important things to consider before paying out any money towards this type of business.

You can also look for other lawsuits that the company has or that the owners may be involved in. Usually a lawsuit indicates fraudulent business practices. It also indicates that the owners have been involved in unscrupulous dealings.

Many of these multilevel marketing schemes do not have a product or service that is business related or anything of value.

Consider this before wasting your money or investing in a multi-level marketing scheme with them. Before investing in any way, research the business, gathering as much pertinent information as you can in order to make a good, solid decision.

If there is anything to reveal, it will be revealed upon research and discovery.

HOME BASED BUSINESSES

The home business scam is prevalent among those who want to be their own boss and work from the comforts and conveniences of home. There is appeal in not having someone to answer to and having the flexibility of being in control.

Spending more time with family, saving the cost of commuting and decreasing expenses is a big deal for the aspiring home business worker who is looking to get started in the home business world.

Know beforehand that true success depends on several things before you get started in the home business venture. Two basic things are needed for a successful home business.

1.) A useful, valuable product or service

2.) A demand for that product or service.

In addition, most home businesses do not succeed because they fail to address the needs of the customer. Sometimes the product is of low quality, and no one wants it. Or perhaps there is so much competition that it is impossible to sell enough of the product or service to make it profitable.

Research the product or service that you want to market before you invest any money into building your business. Thorough research is the best indicator and findings of whether or not your product will succeed.

It will also show you whether or not there is demand for it within existing markets. It will help direct marketing strategies and identify your target customers.

The most important tool that you can ever have for the home business is the use of research. Running a home business IS running a full time business and requires the full use of your attention, time and resources in order to be successful.

Much of the time that is spent in pursuit of a home business is actually getting the business positioned to function efficiently and effectively.

Promoting the business requires a lot of time and effort focused on finding new clients, driving traffic to your websites or in marketing your business via different channels on the web.

There is no doubt that building a business can cost a significant amount of money, much of which is absorbed in start-up costs. These start-up costs are accounted in equipment, supplies, computer inventory, and marketing and promotional materials.

These costs are essential in getting a new business off the ground and into the minds of the consumers that you are trying to reach.

When you decide to start a new business, and you realize the costs that are necessary to make it thrive, you must quickly decide into which veins you will deposit the largest amount of your holdings where it will make a difference.

✓ Should you place the bulk of it into computers and hardware inventory?

✓ Should you heavily market your product or service, thereby substantially increasing your marketing campaigns so that they yield the most favorable results?

✓ What about the actual home office set-up; should you be concerned about the longevity and the practicality of getting the best and the latest equipment for your needs?

Home business costs can easily spiral out of control. The last thing that you as a business needed is to spend some of that savings on a program that makes fantastic promises but may in fact doom your business to failure. Home businesses can work.

Just realize that these so-called programs are often a complete waste of money that could be better spent elsewhere. Don't buy into "instant success" as in reality; it truly takes time to actually make a profit from the home business.

Your best weapon for getting the home business to succeed, once again, is research. So be prepared before entering the home business realm.

What to Do If You Are Scammed

There are things you can do legally if you have been scammed. This first thing to do is contact the bank or your credit card company immediately. Inform them of the situation and they will devise a plan of recompense in order to retrieve the funds.

Gather all of the names of the involved persons and hold on to them for future reference. It is important to do this so as to avoid any future likeliness of the scammers doing this type of behavior again.

It is better to report the incident as soon as is possible so as to avoid the scammer using the stolen credit card again. Since the incident is a lawful offense, chances are that they will get caught but you can help to escalate the incident sooner by being proactive.

There are also cases of identity theft where the person who is violation will likely avoid the law and avoid getting caught. If you are involved in cases of identity theft, there are certain things that you can do to remedy the situation.

First, contact the social security administration, the driver's license administration and the police department in order to file a police report. It will be imminently necessary to get new driver's license, a new passport, and new social security cards.

Basically, it will look and feel as if you are assuming a new identity (almost), but you are working to restore your old identity and to restore any modicum of stability in your life.

It is also important to notify all those parties that are of relevance to your private information that your identity has been stolen and that you are working to restore things as they should be. The more you communicate with them, the less likely the chance is that there will be any future problems.

In addition to all of the legal activity that you will enact to remedy this situation, you will also want to change all of the passwords to your account immediately. This will limit and hopefully eliminate the access to any of your accounts that the scammers may have had.

Also, create new security questions, passwords and access numbers to your accounts in an effort to dissuade any further illegal activity.

If it is possible, you may also want to consider cancelling and re-registering any accounts that may have held any privy information to your accounts. This is actually the best thing you can do to reestablish yourself positively.

In many cases, this may not be doable, but if it is, start over so as to completely wipe out any semblance of old account activity that may be tempting for scammers.

You should also take screen shots of the identity-theft attack, especially if the offense was done on-line.

Screen shots will offer definitive proof that this happened and will give the authorities something more concrete to work with.

If you have proof that a scam took place, via screen shots, you run a much better chance of recouping your lost money or information than if you do not.

To find out how your system was infiltrated, you can invest in and perform an anti-virus program to detect the origination point. Anti-virus programs will help you greatly in recovering your money since they often notate time, occurrence and even what the offense is (i.e., worm, virus, email attacks, etc.).

If this information is able to be identified, you can target your plan of attack and recovery as well. It helps to know how and where something occurred in order to be able to fix it.

In the end, it may be necessary to completely eliminate and reinstitute your hard drive before you are able to rid your system of attack viruses or programs that found their way onto your system's hard drive. If you do have to go to this extreme to remedy your situation, t may

FINDING A LEGITIMATE WORK
FROM HOME JOB

Finding a legitimate, work at home job that pays fair and asks for a fair amount of work can be a long, arduous process.

You must approach it from a perspective of looking at it from a detailed, focused perspective so that you can avoid scams and any hint of jobs that are questionable or those asking you to do unethical things.

As you start your long process of finding that "right job", it may be necessary to look through hundreds, if not thousands of jobs, job boards, leads and referrals before finally deciding on something that is comfortable for you and that feels right.

If you are considering a long term job, a career online and something that you can envision yourself doing ten or twenty years from now, take your time and look diligently for those jobs that are going to give you stability and focus in return for dedicated hard work.

Printed by Libri Plureos GmbH in Hamburg, Germany